OWNER AND COMPANY

NAME: ____
ADDRESS: ____
____
PHONE & EMAIL: ____

COMPANY NAME: ____
BUSINESS ADDRESS: ____
____
PHONE & EMAIL: ____

EMERGENCY CONTACT PERSON: ____
PHONE & EMAIL: ____

INSURANCE COMPANY: ____
AGENT: ____
PHONE: ____
EMAIL: ____
NOTES: ____

LOG BOOK DETAILS

CONTINUED FROM LOG BOOK: ____
LOG START DATE: ____
CONTINUED TO LOG BOOK: ____
LOG END DATE: ____

NOTES / IMPORTANT INFORMATION

____
____
____
____
____
____
____
____
____

ANNUAL MILEAGE SUMMARY

Month	Business Miles	Private Miles	Total
		Total	

Notes

ANNUAL EXPENSES SUMMARY

Month	Fuel	Parking	Tolls	Repairs	Others	Total
Total						

Notes

MILEAGE LOG

Year :	Make :	Model :

Date & Time	Odometer		Total Mileage	Destination	Notes
	Start	End			

EXPENSES TRACKER

EXPENSES					Notes
Fuel	Parking	Tolls	Repairs	Others	

MILEAGE LOG

Year :	Make :	Model :

Date & Time	Odometer		Total Mileage	Destination	Notes
	Start	End			

EXPENSES TRACKER

EXPENSES					Notes
Fuel	Parking	Tolls	Repairs	Others	

MILEAGE LOG

Year :	Make :	Model :

Date & Time	Odometer		Total Mileage	Destination	Notes
	Start	End			

EXPENSES TRACKER

EXPENSES					Notes
Fuel	Parking	Tolls	Repairs	Others	

MILEAGE LOG

Year :	Make :	Model :

Date & Time	Odometer		Total Mileage	Destination	Notes
	Start	End			

EXPENSES TRACKER

EXPENSES					Notes
Fuel	Parking	Tolls	Repairs	Others	

MILEAGE LOG

Year :	Make :	Model :

Date & Time	Odometer		Total Mileage	Destination	Notes
	Start	End			

EXPENSES TRACKER

EXPENSES					Notes
Fuel	Parking	Tolls	Repairs	Others	

MILEAGE LOG

Year :	Make :	Model :

Date & Time	Odometer		Total Mileage	Destination	Notes
	Start	End			

EXPENSES TRACKER

EXPENSES					Notes
Fuel	Parking	Tolls	Repairs	Others	

MILEAGE LOG

Year :	Make :	Model :

Date & Time	Odometer		Total Mileage	Destination	Notes
	Start	End			

EXPENSES TRACKER

EXPENSES					Notes
Fuel	Parking	Tolls	Repairs	Others	

MILEAGE LOG

Year :	Make :	Model :

Date & Time	Odometer		Total Mileage	Destination	Notes
	Start	End			

EXPENSES TRACKER

EXPENSES					Notes
Fuel	Parking	Tolls	Repairs	Others	

MILEAGE LOG

Year :	Make :	Model :

Date & Time	Odometer		Total Mileage	Destination	Notes
	Start	End			

EXPENSES TRACKER

EXPENSES					Notes
Fuel	Parking	Tolls	Repairs	Others	

MILEAGE LOG

Year :	Make :	Model :

Date & Time	Odometer		Total Mileage	Destination	Notes
	Start	End			

EXPENSES TRACKER

EXPENSES					Notes
Fuel	Parking	Tolls	Repairs	Others	

MILEAGE LOG

Year :	Make :	Model :

Date & Time	Odometer		Total Mileage	Destination	Notes
	Start	End			

EXPENSES TRACKER

EXPENSES					Notes
Fuel	Parking	Tolls	Repairs	Others	

MILEAGE LOG

Year :	Make :	Model :

Date & Time	Odometer		Total Mileage	Destination	Notes
	Start	End			

EXPENSES TRACKER

EXPENSES					Notes
Fuel	Parking	Tolls	Repairs	Others	

MILEAGE LOG

Year :	Make :	Model :

Date & Time	Odometer		Total Mileage	Destination	Notes
	Start	End			

EXPENSES TRACKER

EXPENSES					Notes
Fuel	Parking	Tolls	Repairs	Others	

MILEAGE LOG

Year :	Make :	Model :

Date & Time	Odometer		Total Mileage	Destination	Notes
	Start	End			

EXPENSES TRACKER

EXPENSES					Notes
Fuel	Parking	Tolls	Repairs	Others	

MILEAGE LOG

Year :	Make :	Model :

Date & Time	Odometer		Total Mileage	Destination	Notes
	Start	End			

EXPENSES TRACKER

EXPENSES					Notes
Fuel	Parking	Tolls	Repairs	Others	

MILEAGE LOG

Year :	Make :	Model :

Date & Time	Odometer		Total Mileage	Destination	Notes
	Start	End			

EXPENSES TRACKER

EXPENSES					Notes
Fuel	Parking	Tolls	Repairs	Others	

MILEAGE LOG

Year :	Make :	Model :

Date & Time	Odometer		Total Mileage	Destination	Notes
	Start	End			

EXPENSES TRACKER

EXPENSES					Notes
Fuel	Parking	Tolls	Repairs	Others	

MILEAGE LOG

Year :	Make :	Model :

Date & Time	Odometer		Total Mileage	Destination	Notes
	Start	End			

EXPENSES TRACKER

EXPENSES					Notes
Fuel	Parking	Tolls	Repairs	Others	

MILEAGE LOG

Year :	Make :	Model :

Date & Time	Odometer		Total Mileage	Destination	Notes
	Start	End			

EXPENSES TRACKER

EXPENSES					Notes
Fuel	Parking	Tolls	Repairs	Others	

MILEAGE LOG

Year :	Make :	Model :

Date & Time	Odometer		Total Mileage	Destination	Notes
	Start	End			

EXPENSES TRACKER

EXPENSES					Notes
Fuel	Parking	Tolls	Repairs	Others	

MILEAGE LOG

Year :	Make :	Model :

Date & Time	Odometer		Total Mileage	Destination	Notes
	Start	End			

EXPENSES TRACKER

EXPENSES					Notes
Fuel	Parking	Tolls	Repairs	Others	

MILEAGE LOG

Year :	Make :	Model :

Date & Time	Odometer		Total Mileage	Destination	Notes
	Start	End			

EXPENSES TRACKER

EXPENSES					Notes
Fuel	Parking	Tolls	Repairs	Others	

MILEAGE LOG

Year :	Make :	Model :

Date & Time	Odometer		Total Mileage	Destination	Notes
	Start	End			

EXPENSES TRACKER

EXPENSES					Notes
Fuel	Parking	Tolls	Repairs	Others	

MILEAGE LOG

Year :	Make :	Model :

Date & Time	Odometer		Total Mileage	Destination	Notes
	Start	End			

EXPENSES TRACKER

EXPENSES					Notes
Fuel	Parking	Tolls	Repairs	Others	

MILEAGE LOG

Year :	Make :	Model :

Date & Time	Odometer		Total Mileage	Destination	Notes
	Start	End			

EXPENSES TRACKER

EXPENSES					Notes
Fuel	Parking	Tolls	Repairs	Others	

MILEAGE LOG

Year :	Make :	Model :

Date & Time	Odometer		Total Mileage	Destination	Notes
	Start	End			

EXPENSES TRACKER

EXPENSES					Notes
Fuel	Parking	Tolls	Repairs	Others	

MILEAGE LOG

Year :	Make :	Model :

Date & Time	Odometer		Total Mileage	Destination	Notes
	Start	End			

EXPENSES TRACKER

EXPENSES					Notes
Fuel	Parking	Tolls	Repairs	Others	

MILEAGE LOG

Year :	Make :	Model :

Date & Time	Odometer		Total Mileage	Destination	Notes
	Start	End			

EXPENSES TRACKER

EXPENSES					Notes
Fuel	Parking	Tolls	Repairs	Others	

MILEAGE LOG

Year :	Make :	Model :

Date & Time	Odometer		Total Mileage	Destination	Notes
	Start	End			

EXPENSES TRACKER

EXPENSES					Notes
Fuel	Parking	Tolls	Repairs	Others	

MILEAGE LOG

Year :	Make :	Model :

Date & Time	Odometer		Total Mileage	Destination	Notes
	Start	End			

EXPENSES TRACKER

EXPENSES					Notes
Fuel	Parking	Tolls	Repairs	Others	

MILEAGE LOG

Year :	Make :	Model :

Date & Time	Odometer		Total Mileage	Destination	Notes
	Start	End			

EXPENSES TRACKER

EXPENSES					Notes
Fuel	Parking	Tolls	Repairs	Others	

MILEAGE LOG

Year :	Make :	Model :

Date & Time	Odometer		Total Mileage	Destination	Notes
	Start	End			

EXPENSES TRACKER

EXPENSES					Notes
Fuel	Parking	Tolls	Repairs	Others	

MILEAGE LOG

Year :	Make :	Model :

Date & Time	Odometer		Total Mileage	Destination	Notes
	Start	End			

EXPENSES TRACKER

EXPENSES					Notes
Fuel	Parking	Tolls	Repairs	Others	

MILEAGE LOG

Year :	Make :	Model :

Date & Time	Odometer		Total Mileage	Destination	Notes
	Start	End			

EXPENSES TRACKER

EXPENSES					Notes
Fuel	Parking	Tolls	Repairs	Others	

MILEAGE LOG

Year :	Make :	Model :

Date & Time	Odometer		Total Mileage	Destination	Notes
	Start	End			

EXPENSES TRACKER

EXPENSES					Notes
Fuel	Parking	Tolls	Repairs	Others	

MILEAGE LOG

Year :	Make :	Model :

Date & Time	Odometer		Total Mileage	Destination	Notes
	Start	End			

EXPENSES TRACKER

EXPENSES					Notes
Fuel	Parking	Tolls	Repairs	Others	

MILEAGE LOG

Year :	Make :	Model :

Date & Time	Odometer		Total Mileage	Destination	Notes
	Start	End			

EXPENSES TRACKER

EXPENSES					Notes
Fuel	Parking	Tolls	Repairs	Others	

MILEAGE LOG

Year :	Make :	Model :

Date & Time	Odometer		Total Mileage	Destination	Notes
	Start	End			

EXPENSES TRACKER

EXPENSES					Notes
Fuel	Parking	Tolls	Repairs	Others	

MILEAGE LOG

Year :	Make :	Model :

Date & Time	Odometer		Total Mileage	Destination	Notes
	Start	End			

EXPENSES TRACKER

EXPENSES					Notes
Fuel	Parking	Tolls	Repairs	Others	

MILEAGE LOG

Year :	Make :	Model :

Date & Time	Odometer		Total Mileage	Destination	Notes
	Start	End			

EXPENSES TRACKER

EXPENSES					Notes
Fuel	Parking	Tolls	Repairs	Others	

MILEAGE LOG

Year :	Make :	Model :

Date & Time	Odometer		Total Mileage	Destination	Notes
	Start	End			

EXPENSES TRACKER

EXPENSES					Notes
Fuel	Parking	Tolls	Repairs	Others	

MILEAGE LOG

Year :	Make :	Model :

Date & Time	Odometer		Total Mileage	Destination	Notes
	Start	End			

EXPENSES TRACKER

EXPENSES					Notes
Fuel	Parking	Tolls	Repairs	Others	

MILEAGE LOG

Year :	Make :	Model :

Date & Time	Odometer		Total Mileage	Destination	Notes
	Start	End			

EXPENSES TRACKER

EXPENSES					Notes
Fuel	Parking	Tolls	Repairs	Others	

MILEAGE LOG

Year :	Make :	Model :

Date & Time	Odometer		Total Mileage	Destination	Notes
	Start	End			

EXPENSES TRACKER

EXPENSES					Notes
Fuel	Parking	Tolls	Repairs	Others	

MILEAGE LOG

Year :	Make :	Model :

Date & Time	Odometer		Total Mileage	Destination	Notes
	Start	End			

EXPENSES TRACKER

EXPENSES					Notes
Fuel	Parking	Tolls	Repairs	Others	

MILEAGE LOG

Year :	Make :	Model :

Date & Time	Odometer		Total Mileage	Destination	Notes
	Start	End			

EXPENSES TRACKER

EXPENSES					Notes
Fuel	Parking	Tolls	Repairs	Others	

MILEAGE LOG

Year :	Make :	Model :

Date & Time	Odometer		Total Mileage	Destination	Notes
	Start	End			

EXPENSES TRACKER

EXPENSES					Notes
Fuel	Parking	Tolls	Repairs	Others	

MILEAGE LOG

Year :	Make :	Model :

Date & Time	Odometer		Total Mileage	Destination	Notes
	Start	End			

EXPENSES TRACKER

EXPENSES					Notes
Fuel	Parking	Tolls	Repairs	Others	

MILEAGE LOG

Year :	Make :	Model :

Date & Time	Odometer		Total Mileage	Destination	Notes
	Start	End			

EXPENSES TRACKER

EXPENSES					Notes
Fuel	Parking	Tolls	Repairs	Others	

MILEAGE LOG

Year :	Make :	Model :

Date & Time	Odometer		Total Mileage	Destination	Notes
	Start	End			

EXPENSES TRACKER

EXPENSES					Notes
Fuel	Parking	Tolls	Repairs	Others	

MILEAGE LOG

Year :	Make :	Model :

Date & Time	Odometer		Total Mileage	Destination	Notes
	Start	End			

EXPENSES TRACKER

EXPENSES					Notes
Fuel	Parking	Tolls	Repairs	Others	

MILEAGE LOG

Year :	Make :	Model :

Date & Time	Odometer		Total Mileage	Destination	Notes
	Start	End			

EXPENSES TRACKER

EXPENSES					Notes
Fuel	Parking	Tolls	Repairs	Others	

MILEAGE LOG

Year :	Make :	Model :

Date & Time	Odometer		Total Mileage	Destination	Notes
	Start	End			

EXPENSES TRACKER

EXPENSES					Notes
Fuel	Parking	Tolls	Repairs	Others	

NOTES / IMPORTANT INFORMATION

Made in the USA
Monee, IL
16 April 2022

94882106R00066